The Royal School of Church Music

I0171908

Anthems from Worship Songs

16 arrangements by

James Whitbourn

and

Alan Wilson

Copyright Information and Acknowledgements

First published October 1993.

Those who control the copyrights in the music, words and arrangements are identified at the foot of the first page of each item. (Please note that in many cases the RSCM does NOT control the copyright in the works used.) At the time of this printing, the addresses of the copyright controllers known to us were as follows:

Celebration/Thankyou Music - c/o Thankyou Music.

Franciscan Communications Inc., 1229 South Santee Street, Los Angeles, CA90015-2566, USA.

G.I.A. Publications Inc., 7404 S Mason Avenue, Chicago, IL60638, USA.

Integrity's Hosanna! Music - c/o Thankyou Music.

Iona Community/Wild Goose Publications, Pearce Institute, Govan, Glasgow, G51 3UU, UK.

Maranatha Music Inc., administered by Copycare Ltd., 8 Marshfoot Lane, Hailsham, BN27 2RA, UK.

Oxford University Press, Music Department, Walton Street, Oxford, OX2 6DP, UK.

R.S.C.M., Addington Palace, Croydon, CR9 5AD, UK.

Stainer & Bell Ltd., Box 110 Victoria House, 23 Gruneisen Road, London, N3 1DZ, UK.

Thankyou Music, PO Box 75, Eastbourne, BN23 6NW, UK.

We have made every effort to identify all copyright holders and to all of them we are most grateful. We apologise if there are any errors or omissions and we will correct them in future printings.

Originated by Jon English
Reproduced and printed by Halstan & Co. Ltd., Amersham, Bucks.

Contents

Preface

In many ways, the modern 'worship-song' is the new name for 'carol', a term now almost exclusively associated with Christmas. The essential characteristics are all the same: direct and unsophisticated words, set to a simple, folk-like melody which is easily remembered and readily sung.

It was back in 1928, in his Preface to *The Oxford Book of Carols*, that Percy Dearmer, on behalf of Ralph Vaughan Williams and Martin Shaw, made two sound arguments for their newly-collected material:

> *"We think that carols might be continuously sung in ordinary parish churches, where the choir often try to emulate the too difficult anthem of cathedral and collegiate churches...*
>
> *"Perhaps nothing is just now of such importance as to increase the element of joy in religion; people crowd in our churches at the Christmas, Easter and Harvest Festivals, largely because the hymns for those occasions are full of a sound hilarity."*

On both counts, Percy Dearmer's observations seem to have become more true as time has passed. Sound hilarity (as opposed to frivolous hilarity) has proved itself the most Christian and most attractive of qualities. More significantly, the gulf between parish music and cathedral music is now wider than ever before. Few parish musicians nowadays can look to the cathedrals for the most appropriate model on which to base their own endeavours, and few cathedral choirs, with their fixed resource of SATB choir and organ, can easily draw on the new range of parish repertory.

This collection is made solely to bridge that gap, and we hope that these arrangements will be equally useful to any traditional-type choir, developing a call for a breadth of musical style, as to any informal singing group seeking a musical setting for a specific occasion. In no way are any of them intended to be the 'definitive' arrangements, or even an improvement upon the originals. They are merely designed to take their place alongside other versions of the songs and hymns, while catering for a particular group of musicians.

Our purpose differs from the earlier RSCM publication *Sing with all my Soul*, whose aim was to provide interesting arrangements to enhance congregational singing. Our arrangements, on the other hand, are for choirs and singing groups alone, to be used as anthems. We hope they may be enjoyed by those who like to sing special choir arrangements of carols at Christmas, when the familiarity of the tune itself adds to the appeal of the arrangement. We hope they will prove attractive to singers from many traditions, and that they will contribute to the joy and "sound hilarity" of Christian worship all the year round.

1993 James Whitbourn

1. I love the name of Jesus

Words & Melody: Kathleen Thomerson

arr. Alan Wilson

1
With grace and dignity
S/A 1. I
All 3. I
Organ
mf
5
love the name of Je-sus, King of my heart, he is ev - 'ry - thing to me. I
love the name of Je-sus, splen-dour of God, and his face I long to see. I
9
bless the name of Je-sus, reign in my life, show the Fa-ther's love so free.
bless the name of Je-sus, shep-herd of men, by his side I now can be.

13
Spi-rit of love, spi-rit of power, shine through e-ter-ni-ty. I
Spi-rit of love, spi-rit of power, shine through e-ter-ni-ty. I
17
Fine
love the name of Je-sus, light of the world, let me walk each day with thee.
praise the name of Je-sus, for he is love, and that love he gives to me.
20
Verse 2 (preferably unaccompanied)
2. I love the name of Je-sus, ri-sen a-bove, and he loves and prays for
24
me. I bless the name of Je-sus, rul-ing on high, with a glo-rious ma-jes-

28
ty. Spi-rit of love, spi-rit of power, shine through e - ter-ni -

32
D.C. al Fine
ty. I praise the name of Je-sus, Lord of my life, for he died to set me free.

2. A new commandment

Refrain, words of v.1 and tune: Unknown
Words of vv.2-4: Aniceto Nazareth

arr. Alan Wilson

1
With movement and clarity
Refrain
1st time: S/A
2nd time: T/B
A new com-
3
Organ
f
6
mand-ment I give un - to you: that you love one an - o-ther as
11
I have loved you, that you love one an - o-ther as I have loved

16
Solo †
you. 1. By this shall all men know you are my dis -
3. I am the true vine, my Fa - ther is the
20
ci - ples – if you have love one for an - o - ther. By
gard' - ner. A - bide in me: I will be with you. I
25
this shall all men know you are my dis - ci - ples – if
am the true vine, my Fa - ther is the gard' - ner. A -
29
Full
you have love one for an - o - ther.
bide in me: I will be with you. A

† see Performance Notes

33
new — com - mand - ment I give — un - to you: — that you
37
love — one — an - o - ther as I — have loved you, — that you
41
love — one an - o - ther as I have loved you.
2. You
4. True

45
are my friends if you do what I com - mand you. With -
love is pa - tient, not ar - ro - gant nor boast - ful; love
49
3
out my help you can do no - thing. You are my
bears all things, love is e - ter - nal. True love is
54
friends if you do what I com - mand you. With -
pa - tient, not ar - ro - gant nor boast - ful; love

57
3
Dal segno
out my help you can do no - thing.
A
bears all things, love is e - ter - nal.
3
3
61
Last Refrain
Descant (Sopranos)
A new com- mand- ment I give to you: that
Tune (Unison)
new com - mand - ment I give un - to you: that you
65
you love, that you love
love one an - o- ther as I have loved you, that you

69
— one an - o - ther as I— have loved you.
love one an - o - ther as I have loved you.

3. An Upper Room

Words by Frederick Pratt Green
English traditional melody (O Waly, Waly)

arr. James Whitbourn

1
♩ = 76
Organ
p

5
Melody
mf
1. An up - per room did our Lord pre - pare for those he
3. And af - ter sup - per he washed their feet, for ser - vice
Harmony group
p
1. An up - per room did
3. And af - ter sup - per

8
loved until the end: and his dis - ci - ples still ga - ther
too is sa-cra - ment. In him our joy shall be made com -
our Lord pre - pare and his dis -
he washed their feet, In him our
11
there, to ce - le - brate their ri - sen friend.
plete – sent out to serve, as he was sent.
ci - ples still ga - ther there.
joy shall be made com - plete.

14
S
A
mf 2. A last - ing
p 4. No end there
T
B
18
gift Je - sus gave his own – to share his bread, his lov - ing
is: we de - part in peace. He loves be - yond our ut - ter -
21
cup What-ev - er bur - dens may bow us down he by his
most: in ev-ery room in our Fa - ther's house he will be
bow us down he by his
Fa - ther's house he will be

24
1
cross shall lift us up.
there, as Lord and
1
27
2
host.
2
p
dim.

4. Colours of Day

Words & Music: McClellan, Poc & Ryecroft

arr. Alan Wilson

With vigour (one in a bar)
Organ
f
Descant (last verse only)
Ah,
1. S/A
3. Tutti
mf 1. Co - lours of day dawn in - to the mind, the
f 3. O - pen your eyes, look in - to the sky, the
†
Ah,
Ah,
sun has come up, the night is be - hind. Go down in the ci - ty,
dark - ness has come, the sun came to die. The eve - ning draws on, the

† see Performance Notes

19
Ah.
1. T/B
in - to the street, and let's give the mes - sage to the peo - ple we meet. So
sun dis - ap - pears, but Je - sus is li - ving, and his spi - rit is near. So
25
Light up the fire, o - pen the
light up the fire and let the flame burn, o - pen the door, let
light up the fire and let the flame burn, o - pen the door let
†
31
door, let Je - sus re - turn. Take seeds of his spi - rit, let the fruit
Je - sus re - turn. Take seeds of his spi - rit, let the fruit grow; tell the
Je - sus re - turn. Take seeds of his spi - rit, let the fruit grow; tell the

† see Performance Notes

37
grow, let his love show.
peo-ple of Je - sus, let his love show.
peo-ple of Je - sus, let his love show.
43
Fine
Choir
49
2. Go through the park, or in-to the town; the sun still shines
Ah, Ah,
54
on, it ne-ver goes down. The light of the world is ri-sen a - gain; the
Ah,

61
peo-ple of dark - ness are need-ing our friend.
Ah. So light up the
66
fire and let the flame burn, o - pen the door, let
71
Je - sus re - turn. Take seeds of his spi - rit, let the fruit
76
D.C. al Fine
grow, tell the peo-ple of Je - sus, let his love show.

5. I am the Bread of Life

Words & Melody: Suzanne Toolan, SM

arr. Alan Wilson

1
With vigour
Organ
f

Optional rhythmic variation for verse 2

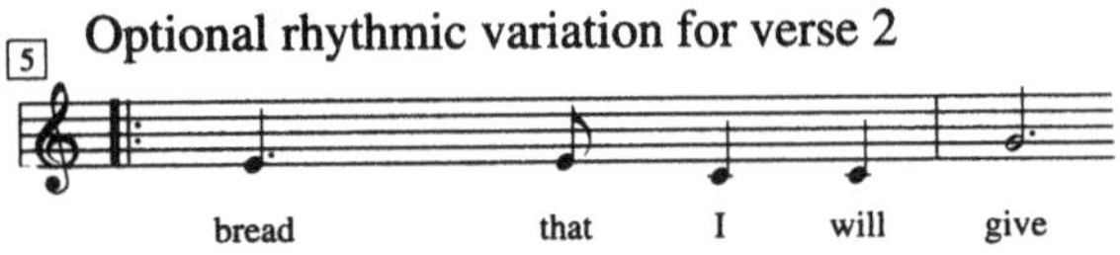
5
bread that I will give

T/B 1. I am the bread of life. He who comes to me shall not
S/A 2. The bread that I will give is my flesh for the life of the

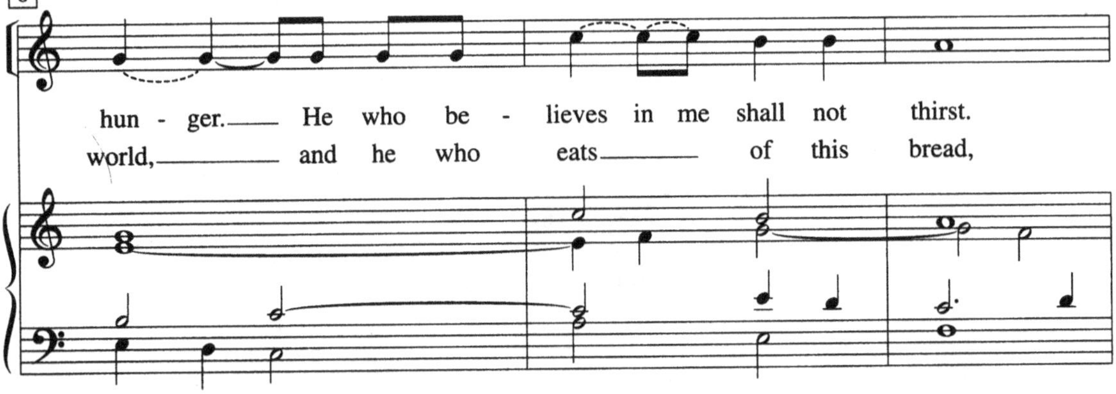
8
hun - ger. He who be - lieves in me shall not thirst.
world, and he who eats of this bread,

11
Tutti
No-one can come to me unless the Father draw him. And I will
he shall live for ever, he shall live for ever. And I will
15
raise him up, and I will raise him up, and I will
raise him up, and I will raise him up, and I will
Optional rhythmic variation for verse 2
S/A
day. 2. The
19
raise him up on the last day.
raise him up on the last day.

23
p Preferably unaccompanied
3. Un - less you eat of the flesh of the Son of Man and drink of his
28
cresc.
blood, and drink of his blood, you shall not have life with - in you. And I will
33
raise him up, and I will raise him up, and I will
37
raise him up on the last day.

41
Unison
5. Yes, Lord, I be - lieve that you are the Christ, the Son ___ of
4. I am the Re - sur - rec-tion, ___ I am the Life. He who be - lieves ___ in
46
God, who ___ has come in - to the world. And I will
me, ___ ev - en if he die, ___ he shall live for ev - er. And I will

51
With clarity
raise___ him up, and I will raise___ him
And I will raise him up, and I will raise him
raise,___ and I will raise___ him up,
raise,___ and I will raise___ him up, and I will
54
up, and I will raise___ him up___ on the
up,___ and I will raise him up on the
and I will raise him up, and I will raise him up on the
raise him up, raise him up, raise him up on the

57
1
2
Coda
ff
last day. day. raise him
ff *
last day. day. And I will raise him
ff
last day. day. And I will raise him
ff
last day. day. And I will raise him
ff
61
up, raise him up, raise him
up, and I will raise him up, and I will raise him
up, and I will raise him up, and I will raise him
up, raise, raise him up, and I will

* plus 2nd sopranos, if preferred.

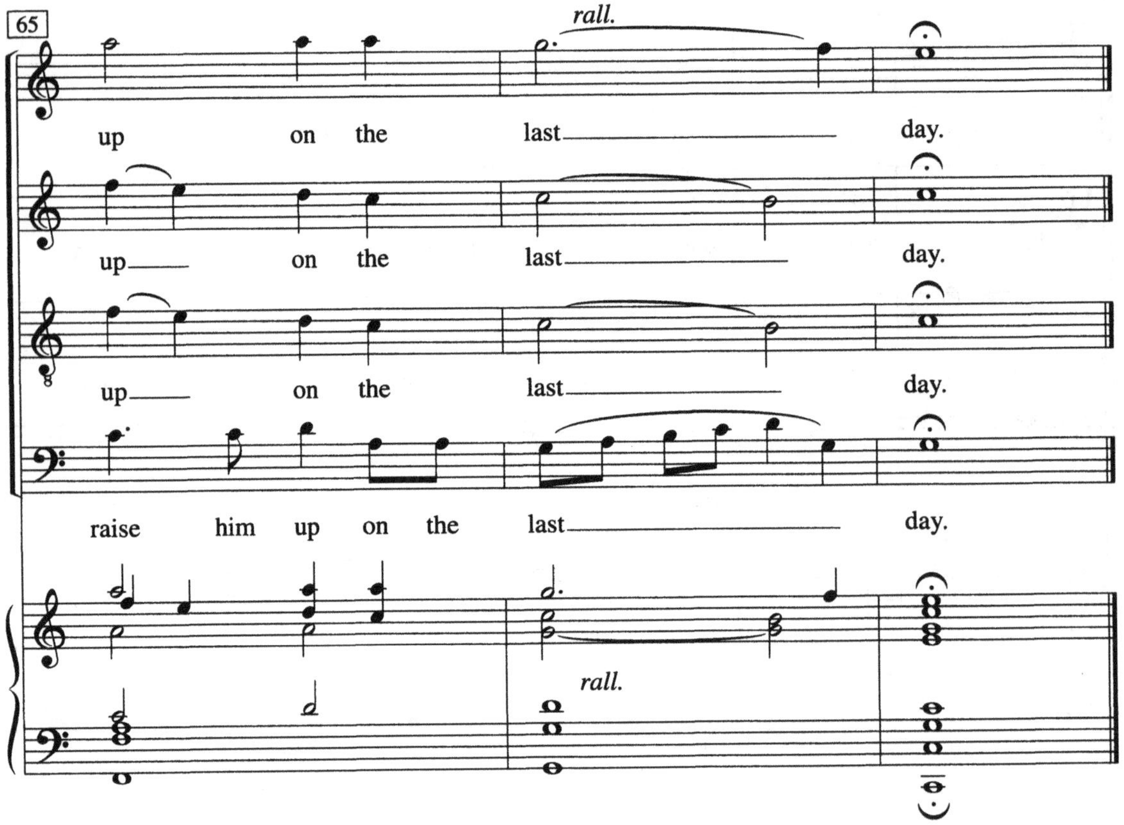
65
rall.
up on the last day.
up on the last day.
up on the last day.
raise him up on the last day.
rall.

6. *Jesus my Lord*

Words by H C A Gaunt
Melody by Cyril Taylor

arr. James Whitbourn

1
♩ = 96
Organ
p
7
p 1. Je - sus my Lord, let me be near you by your own word
(♮)
13
help me to hear you. Je - sus my Lord, lead me to

18
love you, no - thing more dear, no - one a - bove you.
23
mp 2. All through the day
mf 3. Teach us to know
cresc.
dim.
29
sis - ters and bro - thers yours we will be car - ing for
see - ing from blind - ness help us to show ev - 'ry - where

34
oth - ers hear - ing your words learn - ing your
kind - ness. Je - sus our Lord lead us and
38
1
sto - ry.
solo
p
42
p
bear - ing your cross shar - ing your glo - ry.

46
2
guide us.
solo
p
3
man.
51
p
best of all friends always be - side us.
55
p
A - men, A - men.
pp

7. *Give thanks with a grateful heart*

Words & Melody: Henry Smith

arr. Alan Wilson

1
With grace and dignity
Solo Soprano
Piano †
p
Give
5
thanks with a grate-ful heart, give thanks to the Ho-ly One; give
9
thanks because he's given Jesus Christ his Son. Give

† see Performance Notes

13
thanks with a grate - ful heart, give thanks to the Ho - ly One; give
17
thanks because he's gi-ven Je-sus Christ his Son. And
21
now let the weak say "I am strong", let the poor say "I am
25
rich", because of what the Lord has done for us; and

29
now let the weak say "I am strong", let the poor say "I am
33
rich", be-cause of what the Lord has done for— us. Give
37
thanks with a grate - ful heart,— give thanks to the Ho - ly One;— give
p
Ah,
p

41
thanks be-cause he's gi-ven Je-sus Christ his Son. Give
Ah.

45
thanks with a grate - ful heart, give thanks to the Ho - ly One; give
Ah,

49
thanks ___ be-cause he's gi-ven ___ Je-sus Christ ___ his Son.
And
Ah, ___
53
now let the weak say "I am strong", let the poor say "I am
Ah, ___ Ah, ___

57
rich", be-cause of what the Lord has done for_ us.
f (Intense)
Ah. And

61
now_ let the weak say "I am strong",_ let the poor say "I am

65
mf
Give
rich", — be - cause of what the Lord has done for — us. —
69
thanks with a grate - ful heart, — give thanks to the Ho - ly One; — give
73
f
thanks — be - cause he's gi-ven — Je-sus Christ — his Son. And

77
mf
now let the weak say "I am strong", let the poor say "I am
Ah,
81
p
pp
rich", be-cause of what the Lord has done for us.
Ah, Ah.

85
pp
rit.

8. *Master, speak!*

Words by Frances Ridley Havergal
Music by James Whitbourn

1
Lively and flowing ♩ = 63
Organ
mf
4
mf S/A
1. Mas - ter, speak! Thy ser - vant hear - eth,
2. Speak to me by name, O Mas - ter,
7
T/B
Wait - ing for Thy gra - cious word, Long - ing for Thy
Let me know it is to me; Speak, that I may

10
voice that cheer - eth; Mas - ter, let it now be heard.
fol - low fast - er, With a step more firm and free,
13
I am list - ening, Lord, for Thee; What hast Thou to say for
Where the Shep - herd leads the flock In the sha - dow of the
16
p S/A
me?
rock.
Mas - ter, speak! Though least and low - est,
p

19
Let me not un - heard de - part; Mas - ter, speak! For
22
O Thou know - est All the yearn - ing of my heart,
25
p
Know - est all its tru - est need; Speak, and make me blest in -
p
Ped.

28
f All voices
deed.
4. Mas- ter, speak: and
f
cresc.
31
make me rea-dy When Thy voice is tru-ly heard,
With o-bed-ience
35
glad and stea - dy Still to fol-low ev-ery word.
I am list-ening,

39
rall.
Lord, for Thee; Mas-ter, speak! O speak to me!
rall.

9. I will sing, I will sing

Words & Melody: Max Dyer

arr. James Whitbourn

1
♩ = 144
(Bright registration)
Organ
Gr.
mf
Sw.
4
First Voices poco f
1. I will sing, I will sing a song
2. We will come, we will come as one
3. They that sow in tears shall reap
4. If the Son, if the Son shall make
6
unto the Lord, I will sing, I will sing a song
before the Lord, we will come, we will come as one
in joy, they that sow in tears shall reap
you free, if the Son, if the Son shall make

8
un - to the Lord.
be - fore the Lord.
in joy.
you free.
Second Voices
poco f
1. I will sing, I will sing a song
2. We will come, we will come as one
3. They that sow in tears shall reap
4. If the Son, if the Son shall make
p
Optional Harmony group
Al - le - lu - ia, al - le - lu - ia,
p

10
ff
Al-le - lu - ia, Glo-
un-to the Lord. Al-le - lu - ia, glo - ry to the Lord. Al-le-lu-ia, glo-
be-fore the Lord. Al - le - lu - ia, glo - ry to the Lord.
in joy. Al - le - lu - ia, glo - ry to the Lord.
you free You shall be free in - deed.
mp
f
Glo - ry to the Lord. Al - le -
Gr.

13
– ry to the Lord, Al - le - lu, Al - le - lu - ia, glo - ry to the Lord. Al - le -
– ry to the Lord, Al - le - lu, Al - le - lu - ia, glo - ry to the Lord.
– lu - ia, al - le - lu - ia.

16
lu - ia. Glo - ry to the Lord, Al - le - lu - ia, glo - ry to the
Al - le - lu - ia, Glo - ry to the Lord, Al - le - lu - ia, glo - ry to the
Al - le - lu - ia, al - le - lu - ia.

19
1, 2, 3
4
Lord.
Lord.
Al - le - lu - ia.
Al - le - lu - ia.
Al - le - lu - ia.
Gr.
Sw.
mf
ff
Ped.

10. Prayer of St. Francis

Make me a channel of your peace

Melody by Sebastian Temple

arr. Alan Wilson

Unhurried and gentle
Ch. 8 + 2
1
Organ
3
Solo I
mf
1. Make me a chan - nel of your peace. Where
5
there is hat - red, let me bring your love. Where
7
there is in - ju - ry, your par - don, Lord. And

Dedicated to Mrs Frances Tracy

9
where there's doubt, true faith in you.
Sw.
11
Solo II (or S/A)
mf
2. Make me a chan - nel of your
13
peace. Where there's des - pair in life, let me bring
15
hope. Where there is dark-ness on - ly

17
light, and where there's sad - ness ev - er
19
joy.
Tutti (SATB)
3. Oh, Mas - ter, grant that I may nev - er
Gt. (8')
Ch.

21
seek so much to be con-soled as to con -

23
sole, to be un - der- stood as to un - der -

25
stand, to be loved, as to love with all my
27
Solo (or Choir I)
mf
4. Make me a chan - nel of your
Choir II
p
soul.
Ah,

29
peace. It is in par - don - ing that we are
Ah,
31
par - doned, in giv - ing of our - selves that we re -
Ah,

33
ceive, and in dy - ing that we're born to e-ter - nal
Ah.
35
life.
Tutti (with clarity)
f
3. Oh, Mas - ter, grant that I may nev - er
Gt.

37
Solo †
nev - er seek,
seek so much to be con-soled as to con -
39
sole, to be un - der-stood as to un - der -

41
un - der - stand.
stand, to be loved, as to love with all my
43
cresc.
soul.
Gt.
Add
cresc.

45
f
4. Make me a chan-nel of your peace. It
f

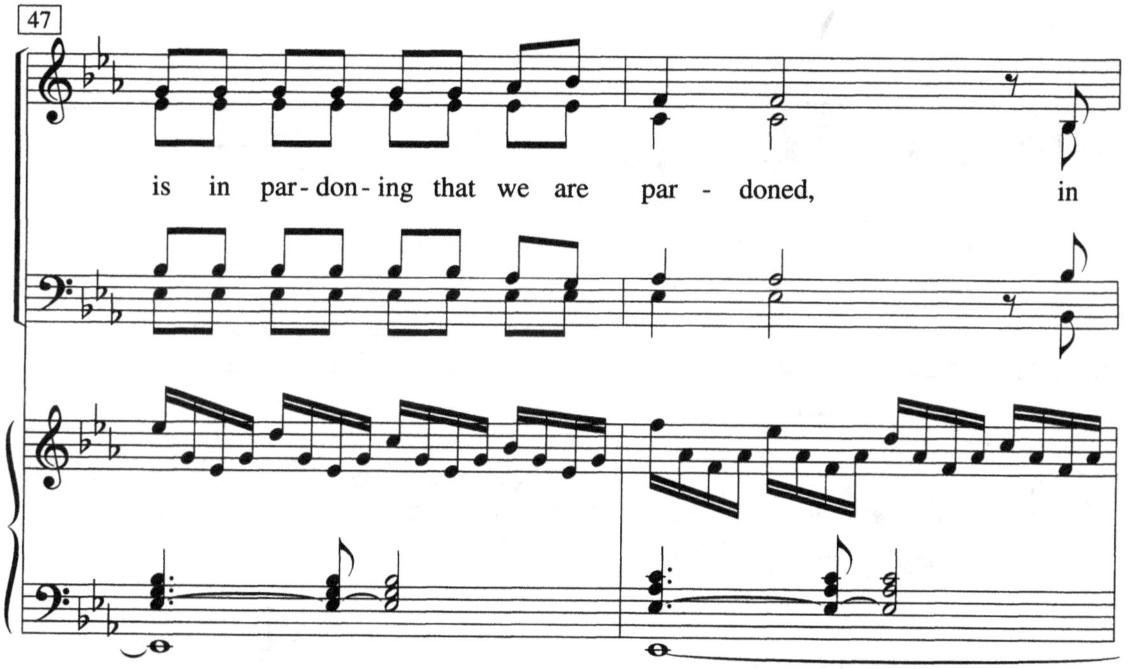
47
is in par-don-ing that we are par - doned, in

49
giv - ing of our-selves that we re - ceive, and in

51
dim.
dy - ing that we're born to e-ter - nal life.

53
meno
mp
Your peace.
Ch.
Ch.
55
meno
p
Your peace.
(Ch.)
Sw.
57
Sw.
pp

11. O breath of life

Words by Elizabeth Head
Melody by Mary Hammond

arr. James Whitbourn

1
𝅗𝅥 = 56
Organ
p
6
S/A
mp
1. O breath of life come sweep - ing through us re - vive thy
4. Re - vive us Lord is zeal a - ba - ting while har - vest
p
10
church with life and power O breath of life come cleanse re -
fields are vast and white? Re - vive us Lord the world is
14
rall. v. 4
Fine
new us and fit Thy church to meet this hour.
wait - ing e - quip Thy church to spread the light.
Fine

18
mp
2. O Wind of God come bend us break us Till hum-bly
p
mm
mm
22
we con - fess our need. Then in Thy ten - der - ness re -
mm
26
make us Re - vive re - store for this we plead.
mm

Melody (S/A)
30
mf
3. O breath of love come breathe with - in us Re - new-ing
mf
Harmony group
ah
ah
34
thought and will and heart.
cresc.
Come, love of Christ a - fresh to
cresc.
ah
cresc.

38
D.C. al Fine
win us Re - vive Thy church in ev - 'ry part.
D.C. al Fine
ah
D.C. al Fine

12. *Seek ye first*

Words & Melody: Karen Lafferty

arr. Alan Wilson

1
Flowing
Piano/
Organ †
mf

5
1. Tenors
2. Sopranos
4. Tenor solo
5. Soprano solo
1. Seek ye___ first the___ king - dom of God,
2. Man shall not live by___ bread___ a - lone,
4. If the___ Son shall___ set___ you___ free,
5. Let your___ light so___ shine be - fore___ men
Choir (vv. 4 & 5 only) †
Ah,

† see Performance Notes

7
and his right - eous - ness,
But by ev - ery word
Ye shall be free in - deed.
That they may see your good works
Ah,
9
and all these things shall be ad - ded un - to you;
That pro - ceeds from the mouth of God,
Ye shall know the truth and the truth shall set you free,
And glo - ri - fy your Fa - ther in heaven,
Ah,

11
al - le - lu, al - le - lu - ia!
Ah,
1. Tenors
2. Sopranos
4. Tenor solo
5. Soprano solo
13
Al - le - lu - ia, al - le -
1. Basses
2. Altos
4. Bass solo
5. Alto solo
Al - le - lu, al- le - lu - ia, al - le - lu, al- le -
Ah,

16
lu - ia, al - le - lu - ia,
lu - ia, al - le - lu, al - le - lu - ia,
Ah.
19
al - le - lu, al - le - lu - ia!
al - le - lu, al - le - lu - ia.

21
mf 3. Ask and it shall be — gi-ven un-to you, — Seek and — ye shall —
f 6. Trust in the Lord with — all — thine — heart, — He shall di-rect thy —
24
find. — Knock and it shall be — o-pened un-to you, —
paths, — In all thy ways ac - know - ledge — Him, —
27
al - le - lu, al - le - lu - ia!

29
Al - le - lu - ia, al - le - lu - ia
Al - le - lu, al-le - lu - ia, al - le - lu, al-le - lu - ia,
33
*
dal segno
al - le - lu - ia, al - le - lu, al-le lu - ia.
al - le - lu, al-le - lu - ia, al - le - lu, al-le - lu - ia.
**

* Top part in last verse ONLY

** Last verse: play minim A in top line (organ)

13. Shalom

Traditional Israeli folk song

arr. Alan Wilson

1
Slow and ethereal
1st time: Solo
2nd time: Tutti
Sha - lom, my friend, sha -
Ch. flute
Organ
(Play LH & Pedals
2nd time only)
†
Sw.
Ped.
4
lom, my friend, sha - lom, sha - lom. The peace of Christ I
8
Dolce
give you to - day. Sha - lom, sha - lom. Sha -
Play

† see Performance Notes

12
lom, my friend, shalom, my friend, sha-lom, sha-lom. The
16
Sha-lom, sha-lom, sha-
peace of Christ I give you to-day. Sha-lom, sha-lom, sha-
Sha-lom, sha-lom sha-
Sha-lom, sha-
20
lom.
lom.
lom.
lom.
Ch.
Sw.
Sw.

14. The Summons

Words by John Bell and Graham Maule
Traditional Scottish melody (Kelvingrove)

arr. James Whitbourn

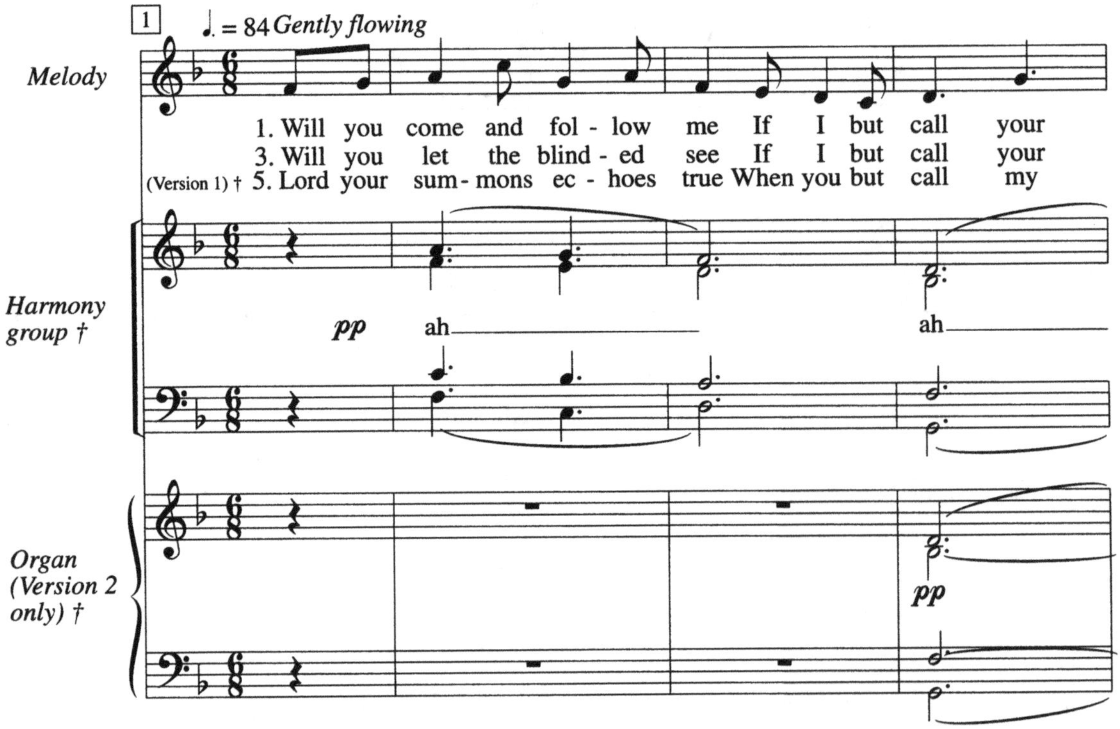
1
♩. = 84 Gently flowing
Melody
1. Will you come and fol - low me If I but call your
3. Will you let the blind - ed see If I but call your
(Version 1) † 5. Lord your sum - mons ec - hoes true When you but call my
Harmony group †
pp
ah
ah
Organ (Version 2 only) †
pp

5
name? Will you go where you don't know And ne - ver be the
name? Will you set the prison - ers free And ne - ver be the
name. Let me turn and fol - low you And ne - ver be the
ah
ah

† see Performance Notes

9
same? Will you let my love be shown, Will you let my name be
same? Will you kiss the lep - er clean And do such as this un -
same. In your com - pa - ny I'll go Where your love and foot - steps
ah
ah

13
last time rall. *
known, Will you let my life be grown, In you and you in me?
seen. And ad - mit to what I mean In you and you in me?
show. Thus I'll move and live and grow In you and you in me.
2. Will you
4. Will you
ah
ah

* Version 1

18
leave your - self be - hind If I but call your
love the "you" you hide If I but call your
(First) Harmony group †
pp mm
Second Harmony group (Version1) or Organ (Version 2) †
pp mm

21
name? Will you care for cruel and kind And ne - ver be the
name? Will you quell the fear in - side And ne - ver be the
mm
mm

† see Performance Notes

25
same? Will you risk the hos - tile stare Should your life at - tract or
same? Will you use the faith you've found To re - shape the world a -
pp ah
ah
pp ah
29
scare? Will you let me an - swer prayer In you and you in me?
round, Through my sight and truth and sound In you and you in me?
mm
mm

34
mf (Version 2 only) †
5. Lord, your summons echoes true When you but call my
mf
38
name. Let me turn and follow you And never be the
42
cresc.
same. In your company I'll go Where your love and footsteps
cresc.
46
rall.
show. Thus I'll move and live and grow In you and you in me.
rall.

† see Performance Notes

15. We cannot measure how you heal

Words by John Bell and Graham Maule

Traditional Scottish melody (Ye banks and braes)

arr. James Whitbourn

1
♩ = 132
Descant 1 (Soprano or instrument) †
Descant 2 (Soprano, tenor or instrument) (v. 3 only) †
Melody (Unison Voices) †
Counter-melody (Men's Voices or bass instrument, eg cello) (vv. 2 & 3 only) †
Organ
p
4
mp
Ky - ri - e e - le - i - son,
mp
Ky - ri - e e -
mf
1. We can - not meas - ure how you heal or
2. The pain that will not go a - way The
3. So some have come who need your help And
mp
2. The pain that will not
3. So some have come who

† see Performance Notes

7
Ky - ri - e e - le - i - son,
le - i - son, Ky - ri - e e -
ans - wer ev - ery suf - f'rer's prayer Yet
guilt that clings from things long past The
some have come to make a - mends As
go a - way The guilt that clings from
need your help and some have come to

9
Ky - ri - e e - le - i - son,
le - i - son, Ky - ri - e e -
we be - lieve your grace res - ponds where
fear of what the fut - ure holds Are
hands which shaped and saved the world Are
things long past, the guilt that clings, the
make a - mends, and some have come, and

11
mf
Ky - ri - e e - le - i - son.
1. Your
2. But
3. Lord
f
le - i - son, e - le - i - son. 3. Lord
f
faith and doubt un - ite to care. 1. Your
pre - sent as if meant to last. 2. But
pre - sent in the touch of friends 3. Lord
mf
guilt that clings to things long past. 2. But
some have come to make a - mends. 3. Lord
13
cresc.
hands though blood - ied on the cross sur -
pre - sent too is love which tends the
let your spi - rit meet us here to
let your spi - rit meet us here to
hands though blood - ied on the cross sur -
pre - sent too is love which tends the
let your spi - rit meet us here to
cresc.
pre - sent too is love which tends the
let your spi - rit meet us here to
f

15
dim.
vive to hold and heal and warn.
hurt we ne - ver hoped to find.
mend the bo - dy mind and soul.
mend the bo - dy mind and soul.
mf
vive to hold and heal and warn To
hurt we ne - ver hoped to find The
mend the bo - dy mind and soul To
dim.
hurt we ne - ver hoped to find
mend the bo - dy mind and soul
17
mp
Ky - ri - e e - le - i - son,
mp
Ky - ri - e e -
car - ry all through death to life and
pri - vate a - gon - ies in - side the
dis - en - tan - gle peace from pain And
mp
The pri - vate a - gon -
To make your peo - ple,

19
Ky - ri - e e - le - i - son.
le - i - son, e - le - i - son.
cra - dle child - ren yet un - born.
me - mo - ries that haunt the mind.
make your bro - ken peo - ple whole.
ies in - side that haunt the mind.
make your bro - ken peo - ple whole.

21
last time
last time
pp

16. When I needed a neighbour

Words & Melody: Sydney Carter

arr. James Whitbourn

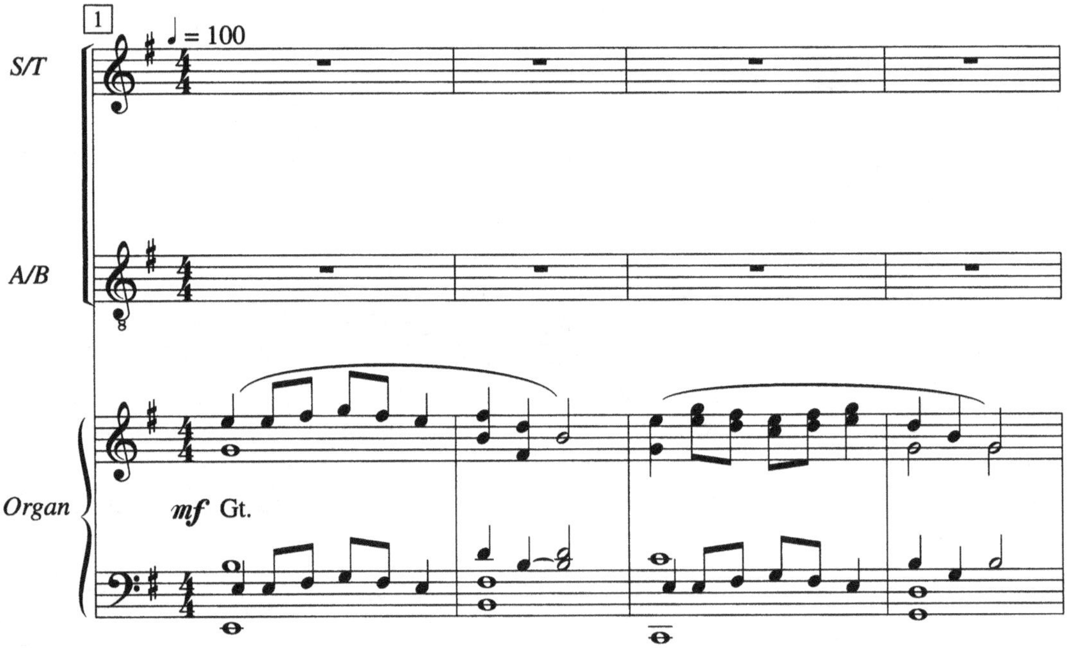
1
♩ = 100
S/T
A/B
Organ
mf Gt.

5
1. When I
need - ed a neigh - bour, were you
hun - gry and thir - sty, were you
cold, I was na - ked, were you
need - ed a shel - ter, were you
Sw. p
(strings)
pp

8
there, were you there? When I need - ed a neigh - bour, were you
there, were you there? I was hun - gry and thir - sty, were you
there, were you there? I was cold, I was na - ked, were you
there, were you there? When I need - ed a shel - ter, were you
10
♩ = 132
there?
there?
there?
there?
And the creed and the co - lour and the
Gt. mf
12
1, 2, 3
name won't mat - ter, were you there?

14
♩ = 100
2. I was
3. I was
4. When I
Sw.
rall.
p
mf
Gt.
17
4
there?
Sw.
pp
mp
Gt.
19
S
A
♩ = 112
mp
5. When I need - ed a heal - er, were you
T
B
mp
tacet
rall.

22
there, were you there? When I need - ed a heal - er were you
24
there? And the creed and the co - lour and the
26
name won't mat - ter, were you there?
molto accel.
mp cresc.

29
rall.
cresc.
ff
33
S/T
♩ = 144
6. Wher -
A/B
♩ = 144
6. Wher - ev - er you tra - vel I'll be
f
36
ev - er you tra - vel I'll be there, I'll be there, wher -
there, I'll be there, wher - ev - er you tra - vel I'll be

38
ev - er you tra - vel I'll be there. And the
there and the creed and the co - lour and the
40
name won't mat - ter, I'll be there.
f
ff
43
ff
And the creed and the co - lour and the
rall.
ff
rall.
45
pp
name won't mat - ter I'll be there.
tacet
pp

Performance Notes

1. I love the name of Jesus

The organ registration should be kept sufficiently mellow in the first verse so as to preserve the sweetness of the S & A voices.

2. A new commandment

The solos on page 9 can be male/female, or groups of voices, or *tutti* sopranos/tenors. Care should always be given to emphasize the refrain and, also, to keep the piece flowing throughout.

3. An upper room

The melody line in verses 1 and 3 may be sung by a solo voice or by a small group of same-pitch voices, but not by a mixed-pitch group. Care should be taken to ensure that the harmony group does not overpower the melody.

4. Colours of day

In verse 1 it would be best to start the introduction reasonably lightly, leaving the pedal out between the "†" signs in bars 9 and 24 to give a gentler accompaniment. This should not, however, be applied to verse 3 where a much richer sound is required, leading up to a very strong sound from bar 42 to the end.

5. I am the bread of life

In this arrangement a nice, brisk tempo is crucial (feeling it as 2 in a bar). Lots of articulation should always be given to "And I will raise him up", especially from page 26 onwards.

6. Jesus my Lord

The organ registration should be delicate and should make use of string-like tones, where available, possibly in combination with a soft stopped diapason. More distinctive sounds should be reserved for the two 'solo' lines (bars 38 - 41 and 46 - 50)

7. *Give thanks with a grateful heart*

Piano is the ideal accompaniment, but careful adaptation for the organ is possible with the pedals holding the bass note on to a minim. Also, piano and organ/synthesizer work well together. The pianist may occasionally want to add extra notes but this must be done with discretion and the graceful style must not be impeded. Instead of solo soprano, a group of children's voices could be used, if preferred.

8. *Master, speak!*

This piece was originally written as a prayer-response, with each verse sung separately, each responding to a spoken prayer. If the music is used in this way, a single bar's introduction (bar 4) should suffice for each response, ending each verse by omitting the linking quavers F♯, G, F♯ in the organ part of bar 16. The accompaniment can be adapted for piano.

9. *I will sing, I will sing*

This piece is best performed with S/A as "First voices" and T/B as "Second voices", if an even-sounding balance is available. If not, two groups of mixed-pitch voices may be used. The optional harmony group is meant as a small 'backing group', and should be sung by a few voices only.

10. *Make me a channel (Prayer of St. Francis)*

On page 52, "Solo 1" should be an alto; page 53, "Solo 2" should be a bass; page 59, the solo should be a soprano (or group of sopranos). From bars 55 to 59, an alternative way of registering the organ part is to reduce the sound of the right hand after each bar, thus producing a *diminuendo*.

11. *O breath of life*

If a flautist is available, the uppermost line of the organ part can be played on the flute throughout. The organist should then omit this line.

12. *Seek ye first*

Like *"Give thanks"*, this is best suited to piano accompaniment and, once again, very tasteful embellishments to the piano part are allowed, including the occasional addition of octaves in the bass. If organ is used, the minim bass notes should be played on the pedals. In bar 5, please note that the choir version should only be used in verses 4 and 5, so as to keep the early part of the piece light in texture. On page 72, verse 3 could be sung *a capella* if so desired; also verse 4, on page 68. The accompaniment could either resume for the "Alleluia" or stay out throughout.

13. Shalom

The solo can be either soprano or high alto, or sung by a group of light-voiced sopranos/trebles. As the right hand on the organ is a flute (the purer the better), the left hand accompaniment sounds good with strings and celestes. Please note that the LH and pedals are not to be played until bar 10 in the first time through.

14. The Summons

Two versions of this piece are provided here. In both versions the melody is sung by a solo voice or a small group of same-pitch voices. I suggest S/A for verses 1, 3 & 5, and T/B for verses 2 & 4.

The harmony parts can be performed by either:

(Version 1) unaccompanied voices. A minimum of 8 singers is required, splitting into two SATB groups for verses 2 & 4.

(Version 2) voices (SATB) and organ. The alternative version of verse 5 should then be used, with all voices singing the melody in unison.

15. We cannot measure how you heal

This piece may be effectively performed in several different ways, but the texture should always build up gradually with the addition of a new part for each verse. It was originally written to be performed in the following way:

verse 1: Melody + Descant 1.

verse 2: Melody + Descant 1 + Counter-melody.

verse 3: All parts together.

The melody may be sung by a group of mixed-pitch voices, whereas the Descant 1 and Counter-melody should be performed at written pitch, and Descant 2 at either a high or low pitch, but not mixed. Care should be taken to ensure that the melody can always be clearly heard.

16. When I needed a neighbour

The four S/A verses (bars 6 - 16) may be sung by a solo S/A voice. A larger organ is desirable for this piece, which demands a wide range of dynamic and tone-colour.

www.ingramcontent.com/pod-product-compliance
Lightning Source LLC
Chambersburg PA
CBHW081634040426
42449CB00014B/3311
* 9 7 8 0 8 5 4 0 2 1 7 1 0 *